A Field Guide to Human Emotions

poems by

Mimi Herman

Finishing Line Press
Georgetown, Kentucky

A Field Guide to Human Emotions

Copyright © 2021 by Mimi Herman
ISBN 978-1-64662-459-1 First Edition
All rights reserved under International and Pan-American Copyright Conventions. No part of this book may be reproduced in any manner whatsoever without written permission from the publisher, except in the case of brief quotations embodied in critical articles and reviews.

ACKNOWLEDGMENTS

Grateful acknowledgments to the editor of *The Iodine Review*, where "Longing" was first published.

Publisher: Leah Huete de Maines
Editor: Christen Kincaid
Cover Art: Bernard D. Herman
Author Photo: John Yewell
Cover Design: Elizabeth Maines McCleavy

Printed in the USA on acid-free paper.
Order online: www.finishinglinepress.com
also available on amazon.com

Author inquiries and mail orders:
Finishing Line Press
P. O. Box 1626
Georgetown, Kentucky 40324
U. S. A.

Table of Contents

Anxiety 1
Baggage 2
Bird in Hand 3
Clutter 4
Condescension 5
Disdain 6
Disquiet 7
Fault 8
Fear 9
Free Time 10
Gossip 11
Homesickness 12
Hope 13
Indignation 14
Insistence 15
Jealousy 16
Longing 17
Need 18
Outrage 19
Ownership 20
Parsimony 21
Passion 22
Passive Voice 23
Perennial 24
Proximity 25
Self-Denial 26
Solitude 27
Stoicism 28
Suppression 29
Trigger Mechanism 30

For John and my family, my companions in this territory, and for Nancy Livingston, who helped me map it.

Anxiety

Anxiety sets its watch ahead
by at least a minute, though often weeks.

Anxiety is one foot in a concrete boot
and the other trying to get away
from someone who is not yet chasing it,
but soon will be. Probably.

Anxiety has an itchy WebMD trigger finger,
which it diagnosed itself.
Anxiety is all about the symptoms.

If you meet anxiety on the street,
be sure to say hello. Otherwise
it will spend all day wondering
if it's done something to alienate you.

Anxiety is the bastard child of terror
and dithering. Abandoned by its father
and raised by its mother,
people mistake it for an idiot,
but it knows more than you think.

Anxiety will never intentionally deceive you,
though it has been known
to be mistaken.

Baggage

Here, a matched set of personal baggage
passed down through generations,
monogrammed, finely stitched,
sold at a cut rate due to insufficient airing
and lengthy storage in extreme climates,
slightly mildewed, but still functional,
carried (until recently) to every destination,
impossible to miss at the baggage carousel.
No wheels—you'll have to lug it yourself—
but you won't find this level of workmanship
in the baggage you've carried for years.
Original owner, priceless, yours for the taking.

Bird in Hand

The bird resists.
It pecks at your palm.
Trust consists
in keeping it there.
Your insistence
that bird in hand
beats two in the bushes
explains the way we understand
that wanting what we have
no matter how it eats at us
outstrips a thousand wishes.

Clutter

Clutter is what you can't get rid of.
It accumulates in your absence.
In your presence it multiplies,
eyes bare spaces,
leaps from shelf to shelf.
It is itself an example
of the commutative property.
It stops at nothing.
Clutter abhors a vacuum.
It aches for company,
is irresistible to dust.
It must want something
you can't afford to give.
It lives to become more so
or so it seems.
Clutter never gleams.
It is too subtle.

Condescension

Condescension loves an echo,
wears platform shoes to dinner parties.
with guppies swimming in the soles,
prefers the balcony box for operas,
buys extra tickets, then sits surrounded
by empty seats.

Condescension hates to date,
prefers the following day's dissection
in the company of friends
who can be derided later.

For condescension, the latest fashion
goes stale as soon as it hits the skin.
Where condescension deigns to dine
the critics swarm around the table,
napkins poised to catch the drips,
mouths agape for morsels dropped.

Disdain

Disdain strides across a sidewalk square
and, if the occasion demands, a city block.
Go ahead and scurry. You can't keep up.
Strangers open doors,
hold elevators, split conversations
to allow it to pass between them.
Disdain does not have to sign in,
make appointments or call ahead.
No one ever put disdain on hold.
Spend five minutes in disdain's company
and you will shrink by inches,
a lifetime, and you'll disappear.

Disquiet

The bed sweats.
The sky splits.
The air is so thick
you could spread it
between your sheets.

All week you've been waiting
for the weather to ease
as if there were some season
we could call neutral.

But weather is a keyboard
built of flats and sharps,
melodic riffs, the heavy bass
on nights like this,
the way two notes
may seem too close,
and discord haunt your dreams.

Fault

I never know where fault will be found
so spend most days scurrying
around the rooms of my intention
with brooms so thickly rushed that—
with absolute attention—
the dust in every corner
can be extracted, every comma splice
repaired, each email answered within minutes,
all the chairs squared with their tables,
all the tables neatly completed,
the numbers adding up to pi,
the pie perfectly browned, the filling
moist, the round 360s,
the straights aligned,
the ocean's natural waves restored,
the stores stocked, the stock herded
with no strays, no stray hairs
growing from chin or upper lip,
no strays slipping off the cliff,
the cliff fenced, the fencers masked
for safety, the safety on, the gun
unloaded, like the groceries, put away
like criminals, the criminal intent
averted like the eyes of children
in the face of evil,
which is what it usually seems to me
any carelessness might lead to.

Fear

Fear is the house special today: thick dust on a fragile plate.
Heavy, sodden, lumpy, spongy. My fork sinks,
then sticks. If I turn away, say it is inedible,
determination pushes in my chair, presses my chest
to the table. No dessert until you finish every bite.
Every bite clogs my swallow, makes me queasy.
Fear sits in my stomach like swamp mud for days
after the flood has receded.

Free Time

It gathers under your bed like dust rats
and whispers superciliously
about how much you've already wasted
before you've opened your eyes.

Your anticipatory sleep last night was exhausting.
The recriminations of your dreams
accused, judged and sentenced
between blinks of your closed eyes.
The entire courtroom, even the reporters
knew you as a recidivist, inclined
to waste whatever time you've stolen.

You can't save minutes for a rainy day.
They must be spent, though probably unwisely
and never as you intended
in your rational budgeting the day before,
when you thought you were rich with time,
but still allotted specific hours for certain tasks.

Now you've squandered them
on the cat sleeping in your lap,
the papers you've redistributed
in piles around your office,
the closet that won't surrender
anything worth wearing,
the movie you've seen so many times
each line echoes in advance.

By the end of the day, you're exhausted.
So much freedom, so little time.

Gossip

Like mildew on lemon
it spreads, pushing toward the edges.
Spores replicate in the crevices
feeding on damp philosophies
of iterative retribution.
With a thin dismissive powder
it stains the hand that lifts it
out of the bowl, whispers
with the candy wrappers,
greasy with sweetness,
when it finds itself in the bin,
spreading its pale green message
even as it decomposes.

Homesickness

The longer I'm away from home
the thinner I become,
transparent, like film,
until I cannot tell a whim
from a wish. Unleash
the dogs, they'll find nothing,
only the scent of me,
the ill-content of me,
the where-she-went of me.

Hope

Hope is subject to erosion,
but slides downstream, while deposition
builds up more on other banks.
The love you left there like a mountain,
the highest point of elevation,
over years will curve and soften.

Indignation

Indignation perches on the edge of a flat city roof
and drums its heels against the brick.
To trick indignation is to incur it.
It has the best view, the only view.
With binoculars, indignation can focus
on a single window, zoom in between the slats
of venetian blinds. Other times, it waves a hand
to show you it means *the whole damned city*.
If you try to help it down to the ground floor,
indignation will suddenly grow heavy,
insist you leave it alone. Forget the weather.
Sleet feeds it. A stiff breeze is just what it needs
to resist your attempts at comfort or conciliation.

Insistence

Insistence doesn't have to beg
when it meets resistance.
It knows exactly what it wants,
knows that it deserves it.
Insistence is a steady beat
on a thinning drumhead,
relentless, but not endless.
It stops seconds
after you surrender.
It is the force under
every geological shift.
It is the knock at the door
that rearranges your day.

Jealousy

Jealousy is a tapeworm.
You start by swallowing it.
It settles, dark and warm, in your intestines
won't come out with the other excreta,
consumes everything you eat,
before you can extract any nutrients,
bloating your guts as it stretches out,
twisting its indigestible length
until it's entirely at home in your body
and you are not.

Longing

Who put the long in longing?
Who decided its most persistent quality
is that it lasts
far beyond the time you wish it were past?

Whose plan was this:
that it should stretch both time and you
to a thinness that makes time wiry and resilient
and you translucent?

And what idiot put the fast in fasting,
when it's nothing like fast,
when just like the length in longing,
it lasts?

In this last fast, the longing for you lasted
until it became the memory of hunger,
and finally, the memory of memory.

Need

Slide me into the pockets
between minutes.
Let me hang on to your breaths
as you drift toward sleep.
I am deft at catching
even the fingertips
of handholds as you fly by.
If there's no time,
I will burrow into the milliseconds
you leave behind.

Outrage

Don't take outrage to a party.
It will yell at the hostess
and leave her wondering
if she wore the wrong dress, or worse,
why she invited you at all.
Outrage wears flounces, but only
in the severest black broadcloth,
takes stiff, thick steps to the bar
then refuses to order,
waits for the bartender
to make the wrong guess,
snatches the drink and knocks it back,
then slams the glass on the marble bar.
Outrage spits half-chewed canapés
into cocktail napkins, insists
you call a cab, then decides to stay anyway
to offend all your friends
who have begun to wonder
what has become of you.

Ownership

How do you take the mine
out of the things you think you own?
Remove the canaries, the drills, the elevators, the glaring lights,
pull up the ladders, seal the shaft with cement, cap all the entrances and exits,
but still it's you, foreman and owner.
It's your mine.

You try to be Buddhist, let go
of objects and people and places.
You tap them with a forefinger
and send them sailing across the sky
to dissipate into rain,
but what of the conservation of mass,
the way the water cycle of your thoughts insists
that they run off and gather,
evaporating to cloud your brow again?

Parsimony

Parsimony
often means
making do with less.
At its worst
it's exponential
like the farmer
with his horse.
Every day
he fed it half
the hay and oats
of the day before.
When finally,
he'd weaned it down
to slivers each
of oats and hay,
the damned ungrateful
stupid horse
up and passed away.
The farmer said
he was surprised
his horse had died.
Tyrants often are.

Passion

The way a wave spirals
with you inside it, the cake
in a jelly roll of fish and shells
is like love when you believe it to be
a force that overtakes you.
You think you drown, then
your head is crowning the crests
and the wave sends you foamed
to the beach, breathless,
fingers outstretched. You clutch
hands full of damp sand, reach
for driftwood to keep you
landed, but still you wish
you could be swept back, roiled above
an ocean floor you cannot touch.

Passive Voice

It has been decided by me
that to take an active role in my life
is not something that should be done.

Therefore, bed is a place
from which I shall not be removed
until such a time
when the necessity has been made clear.
And dear—if that is what you are to me,
henceforth I will be made happy
to be loved by you.

If it should be decided by you
that love is something
that should be made by us
pleasure is something to which
I would be willing to accede,
and if pleasure
should find itself exploding from my being
it is to be hoped
that it will be understood
that in this, as in all things
I am yours.

Perennial

The daffodil insists
on being born
no matter
what the weather.

Trees persist
in leafing,
grass repeating
the same old standards
year after year.

Paint keeps peeling,
runners stealing.

All I own
is planted
in your dirt.
With you
I take rebirth
for granted.

That's how
love works.

Proximity

As we cool, we contract:
ice cubes shrinking away
from the edges
of the tray,
lovers
pulling back.

When we warm
we expand
until a woman in love
hardly needs to move
to stand by her man.

Self-Denial

Dear do for others,
How is it that I can't resist you?
I think I can take one drink,
but that first sip is laced with need.
Even as I swallow, it begins
its escalation through my bloodstream.
As soon as I'm down the stairs,
I come crawling back,
eager to bathe your filthy feet.

By the end of the first week,
I'm sleeping less,
writing lists in my head
of how I can please you
and why I'm not worthy.

If I last a month before I collapse,
I've given up sleep, along with food.
You consume me until I'm a sliver
thinking of how much more I can offer.

Solitude

Solitude begets
solitude
the way a little
begets less.

An allergy
to company
intrudes
with every guest.

Stoicism

The stoic is not a fan of landscapes
with points of interest or rugged terrain,
tolerates mesas, endures hills,
but prefers a plain that stretches
to the edges of the earth,
would rework globes to flatten curves,
has two paces: trudge or stride.

Even vanilla provides more flavor
than the stoic ever orders.
All the stoic's clothes are beige,
hung on hangers in dark closets
with corners swept for doubt or glee.

Interview the stoic's neighbors
and you'll find the deep disorders
not permitted in the house
which pock the yard in small eruptions
underneath the family's footing.

Suppression

Just try it. Emotion will out.
Plaster over anger, and like magma,
it finds another crack in the crust.
Rage, seething, looks for thin spots,
while disapproval, glacial, pushes granite
across the formerly fertile landscape.

Nothing you suppress will stay where you left it.

Trigger Mechanism

The trigger mechanism inside a gun,
inside a lock, inside some
of the people you know,
determines what will set them off.

When we say *defense mechanism*
we mean a person always acts
the same way in similar circumstances.

I like dependability, the ways
locks and keys and some of these
people always act the same.
I take a certain satisfaction
in the expectable chain reaction.

So it brings me to my knees
when a gun misfires,
when locks freeze,
when I desire reliability
in your reactions
and you go off
another way.

MIMI HERMAN is a writer, Kennedy Center teaching artist and member of the AWP Board of Directors. The 2017 North Carolina Piedmont Laureate, she is also a Hermitage Artist Retreat Fellow and an alumna of the Warren Wilson MFA Program for Writers.

Mimi has performed her fiction and poetry at *Why There are Words* in Sausalito, Symphony Space in New York, and Memorial Auditorium in Raleigh, North Carolina. Her writing has appeared in *Michigan Quarterly Review, Shenandoah, Crab Orchard Review, The Hollins Critic, Prime Number* and other journals. She is co-director of Writeaways writing workshops in France, Italy and New Mexico. You can find her at www.mimiherman.com and www.writeaways.com.

www.ingramcontent.com/pod-product-compliance
Lightning Source LLC
LaVergne TN
LVHW041505070426
835507LV00012B/1350